THE STORY OF
Christmas

THE STORY OF
Christmas

The Birth of Jesus
in Scripture and Song

EDITED BY

GARY C. WHARTON

Cumberland House Publishing
Nashville, Tennessee

Published by Cumberland House Publishing, Inc.
431 Harding Industrial Drive
Nashville, TN 37211
www.cumberlandhouse.com

Project editors: Rebecca S. Humm, Sarah M. Hupp, John Mitchell
Cover design by Gore Studio, Inc.

Library of Congress Cataloging-in-Publication Data
  The story of Christmas : the birth of Jesus in Scripture and song / edited by Gary C. Wharton.
      p. cm.
  Includes index.
  ISBN 1-58182-303-7 (pbk.)
  1. Christmas. 2. Jesus Christ—Nativity.   I. Wharton, Gary C., 1940-
  BV45 .S855 2002
  232.92—dc21

                                                                                2002009207

Printed in Canada
1 2 3 4 5 6 7 8 — 06 05 04 03 02

TABLE OF CONTENTS

THREE GOSPEL WRITERS—MATTHEW, LUKE, AND JOHN—
INTRODUCE CHRIST AND TELL OF HIS BIRTH AND
CHILDHOOD. THE FOLLOWING ACCOUNT PRESENTS
THIS NARRATIVE IN CHRONOLOGICAL ORDER.

PREFACE

JESUS CHRIST, the Messiah, is the single most important and influential person in history. Everything, including our yearly calendar, focuses on him and his coming into our world.

The focus of Christmas, of course, is Christ. Most of us are familiar with many elements of the Messiah's birth. We have seen Christmas pageants, sung Christmas carols, and celebrated Christ's manger birth. But many of us would find it difficult to recount the entire narrative of Christ's birth in chronological detail.

The Story of Christmas provides that solution. Taken directly and entirely from the words of Scripture, this newly revised edition synthesizes the gospel accounts of Matthew, Luke, and John and offers a pure, chronological retelling of the birth of Jesus Christ. Believing that God through his Spirit inspired every word of Scripture, *The Story of Christmas* recounts this incredible miracle word-for-word from the Bible without embellishment. Different translations in today's vernacular have been blended together to form this narrative. Only where clarification is required or where there is awkwardness or redundancy between the gospel writers have words been omitted or altered. In addition, appropriate Old Testament prophecies are included to demonstrate the absolute marvel of Christ's miraculous birth.

Poetry and prophecy are presented in open verse for emphasis and beauty, and contemporary language is used throughout, including the personal pronouns for deity (*you* instead of *Thou*, for example). *Holy Spirit* rather than *Holy Ghost* is consistently used, and, in many instances, the Hebrew word *Messiah* is selected over the Greek synonym *Christ*.

In addition, many favorite Christmas carols are added to further celebrate Christ's coming as the miracle baby of Christmas. Historical annotations accompany many of these carols, bringing added inspiration and wonderment to the story of his birth.

It is our prayer that the contemporary narrative and inspirational carols contained in *The Story of Christmas* may provide not only a harmony of the full gospel record, but also bring joy to our hearts as we celebrate Christ's birth and better understand the impact of his life on ours.

What Is a Carol?

The word *carol* is derived from the archaic word *carola* meaning ring dance, an ancient form of sacred folk music dating from the middle ages. Between the scenes of the early mystery and miracle plays which were widely used by the medieval churches for teaching religion lessons, carols were sung and danced—much like today's orchestra performing between the scenes of a drama production.

Today these carols, played between the scenes of our busy lives, continue to teach us, containing within them the full story of God's full plan of redemption.

John Wesley, in his 1739 **Hark! The Herald Angels Sing**, for example, offers a condensed course in biblical doctrine set in poetic form, so that all who sing the carol would be able to embrace the redemptive and reconciling mission that began with the birth of the baby Jesus.

—The Editor

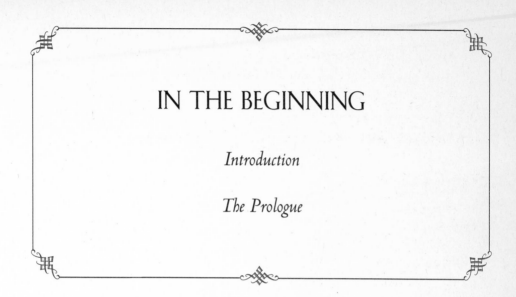

IN THE BEGINNING

Introduction

The Prologue

O Sanctissima

O thou joyful, O thou wonderful
Grace revealing Christmastide!
Jesus came to win us
From all sin within us;
Glorify the Holy Child!

O thou joyful, O thou wonderful
Love revealing Christmastide!
Loud hosannas singing
And all praises bringing:
May Thy love with us abide!

O thou joyful, O thou wonderful
Peace revealing Christmastide!
Darkness disappeareth,
God's own light now neareth:
Peace and joy to all betide!

— Johannes D. Falk;
included in *Tatersall's Psalmody*, 1794

INTRODUCTION

FOLLOWING what was heard by the original eyewitness and servants of Jesus Christ, the Messiah, who is the Word, many have undertaken to compile a narrative of the events that happened among us.

For this reason, I have carefully checked everything from the beginning, and present it here in proper chronological order for you, so that you can be assured that what you have been taught is indeed true.

LUKE 1:1-4

Of the Father's Love Begotten

Of the Father's love begotten,
Ere the worlds began to be,
He is Alpha and Omega,
He the Source, the Ending He.
Of the things that are, that have been,
And that future years shall see,
Evermore and evermore.

O ye heights of heav'n, adore Him;
Angel hosts, His praises sing,
Pow'rs dominions, bow before Him
And extol our God and King.
Let no tongue on earth be silent;
Every voice in concert ring,
Evermore and evermore.

— Aurelius Prudentius;
translation by John M. Neale;
Henry W. Baker, 1859

THE PROLOGUE

BEFORE TIME BEGAN, Jesus Christ lived. In fact, he has always been. In the beginning he was the Word, and as the Word he was with God and he was also God. He was in the beginning eternal with God.

Everything that was created came into being by him and there is nothing in existence that he has not created. In him was life and that life brought light to men. His light shines brightly in the darkness and the darkness cannot snuff it out.

There was a man, sent from God, named John. John came to announce to everyone that this unquenchable light was even then, at that very moment, coming into the world. His purpose in coming was that everyone might believe through him. John was not that light, but he was the announcer of the light's coming.

Jesus Christ is the true light, who, coming into the world, enlightens every man. He was in the world, and even though he had created the world, it did not recognize him.

He came to his own people, and even they did not receive him. But to others who did receive him—those who believed and put their faith in him—to them he gave the right to become children of God. This did not happen through ancestry, nor sexual passion, nor by willing it to be, but by God.

The Word, Jesus, became a human being and lived very briefly among us. We actually saw his glory, the splendor of the only son God ever fathered, the embodiment of all grace and truth.

When John had announced his coming he said, "This was he of whom I said: He who succeeds me has a higher rank than I, for he existed before me."

And from his fullness we have all received bounty heaped upon bounty, because while the law has come to us through Moses, grace and truth came through Jesus Christ.

No man has ever seen God, but he has been revealed to us through the only fathered son, who has now returned to his Father's side.

JOHN 1:1-18

BEFORE JESUS' BIRTH

The announcement of John's birth

The angel's announcement to Mary

The angel's announcement to Joseph

Elizabeth's song

Mary's song

The birth of John the Baptist

Love Has Come!

Love has come—a light in the darkness!
Love explodes in the Bethlehem skies.
See, all heaven has come to proclaim it;
Hear how their song of joy arises:
Love! Love! Born unto you a Savior!
Love! Love! Glory to God on high.

Love is born! Come share in the wonder;
Love is God now asleep in the hay.
See the glow in the eyes of His mother;
What is the name her heart is saying?
Love! Love! Love is the name she whispers;
Love! Love! Jesus, Immanuel.

Love has come—He never will leave us!
Love is life everlasting and free.
Love is Jesus within and among us;
Love is the peace our hearts are seeking.
Love! Love! Love is the gift of Christmas;
Love! Love! Praise to You, God on high.

— Ken Bible

THE ANNOUNCEMENT OF JOHN'S BIRTH

DURING THE REIGN of Herod the Great, who was then king of the Jews, there lived in the province of Judea a priest of the order of Abijah, whose name was Zacharias.

His wife was called Elizabeth, and they shared a common ancestor, the High Priest Aaron. They were a deeply religious couple, devout and zealous in the practice of their faith.

The major disappointment in their lives was that they were childless because of Elizabeth's infertility, and both were now well advanced in years.

It was common practice among the Abijah priests, when it was their turn to serve in the temple, to draw lots determining which duties each would undertake. On this particular day it was Zacharias' responsibility to go into the temple to burn incense. The usual crowd of worshipers remained outside, praying.

In the midst of his duties, Zacharias was suddenly startled with terror. To the right of the altar he saw an angel, the angel of the Lord, who spoke to him!

"Do not be afraid, Zacharias, your prayers have been heard. Elizabeth, your wife, is going to have a son and you are to name him John.

"He will be your joy and delight;
His birth will be a time of great celebration,
    because he is destined to become
    one of God's great men.
He will never touch wine or liquor:

Instead he will be filled
    with the Holy Spirit,
    even in his mother's womb,
    before he is born!
He will be a messenger of God,
    a forerunner of the One
    who is promised to come,
    with the strength and power
    of the prophet Elijah.
He will return many of Israel's children
    to the Lord their God,
And reconcile parents and their children,
    and restore the rebellious
    to the wisdom of the righteous
    to thoroughly prepare his people
    for the coming of the Lord."

"But I am an old man," Zacharias said, "and Elizabeth is getting on in years. How can I be sure this is true?"

"I am Gabriel," the angel replied. "I come directly from standing in the presence of God. I have been sent to speak to you and to bring you this good news. But you do not believe me!

"So from now until all I have said has happened, you will lose your ability to speak, and will remain silent. Put your faith in God, Zacharias. Everything I have told you will come true, at the proper time."

In the meantime, the crowd waiting outside for Zacharias was growing impatient, wondering why he was delayed so long in the sanctuary. When he finally did come out, they immediately realized he had seen a vision. He was unable to speak a word! When he tried to speak, no sound came out. He just stood there, communicating with gestures, but unable to say a word.

So when his duties in the temple were over, he went home. Soon after this, Elizabeth became pregnant, but she did not show herself in public, or tell anyone, for five months.

When she did make the announcement, she said: "This is what the Lord has done for me! God has shown me his favor. He has removed the embarrassment I felt for being childless, and I no longer have to feel ashamed any more."

LUKE 1:5-25

"Behold, I will send you
Elijah the prophet
  before the great and dreadful
  day of the Lord:
And he will turn the heart of the
fathers to the children,
  and the heart of the children to
  their fathers."

By the prophet Malachi, c. 430 B.C.
MALACHI 4:5-6

THE ANNOUNCEMENT TO MARY

AT THE SAME TIME, a virgin whose name was Mary lived in the town of Nazareth, in the province of Galilee. Mary was Elizabeth's cousin, and was engaged to Joseph, a direct descendant of David, the ancient King of Israel.

When Elizabeth was in the sixth month of her pregnancy, God sent the angel Gabriel to Mary. Gabriel entered Mary's room.

"Greetings, Mary," the angel said. "How favored you are. The Lord is with you!"

Startled, Mary tried to comprehend just what such a greeting meant.

"There is no need to be frightened," the angel said. "God loves you very much, and he has chosen you! You are going to have a baby! A son! You are to name him Jesus.

> "He will be great:
>   and he will be called
>   the Son of the Most High God!
> And the Lord God will place him
>   on the throne of his ancestor David.
> He will reign
>   over the house of Jacob forever;
>   and there will never be an end to his reign."

"How can that be?" Mary asked. "I am not married, and I am a virgin."

The angel answered her:

"God's Holy Spirit will envelope you;
    and the power of the Most High God
    will overshadow you;
And your child will be called the Son of God!
Consider your cousin, Elizabeth,
    the one they called the Barren One!
She has conceived in her old age
    and is now pregnant in her sixth month!
    God's promises can never fail!
    There is nothing that God is unable to do.
    Nothing is impossible with God!
    God can do anything!"

"I am the Lord's servant," Mary replied. "Let it happen as you have said."
At that, the angel left her.

LUKE 1:26-38

**"The Lord himself
    will give you a sign;
Behold, a virgin shall conceive,
    and bear a son,
    and shall call his name
Immanuel,"**
(meaning *God with us*).

By the prophet Isaiah, c. 700 B.C.
ISAIAH 7:14

Charles Wesley was the son of an Anglican minister from Epworth, England. After experiencing his own spiritual renewal, Wesley became an enthusiastic preacher who used every opportunity to share his faith, whether in the pulpit or on a street corner. As a means of sharing the gospel message, Wesley set scripture passages to music in hymn form. He ultimately penned more than 6,500 hymns, eighteen of them related to Christmas.

Charles Wesley's Christmas hymns and carols give us a glimpse of the babe in the manger, but they also tie in the greater message of Christ's birth as the Savior of the world, the King of creation, and the fulfillment of long-awaited prophecies. *Come, Thou Long Expected Jesus* embraces the prophecies of Malachi and Haggai, reminding us that "the desire of all nations" (Haggai 2:7) has come in the birth of Jesus Christ the Messiah.

Woven throughout the retelling of the gospel story in each of Wesley's carols is a life-changing lesson. *Come, Thou Long Expected Jesus* is no exception. Wesley's lyrical message reminds us that if we let the manger babe rule our hearts, we can be set free from our fears and sins and find our eternal rest in God.

Come, Thou Long Expected Jesus

Come, Thou long expected Jesus,
Born to set Thy people free;
From our fears and sins release us;
Let us find our rest in Thee.

Israel's strength and consolation,
Hope of all the earth Thou art;
Dear Desire of every nation,
Joy of every longing heart.

Born Thy people to deliver,
Born a child and yet a king.
Born to reign in us forever,
Now Thy gracious kingdom bring.

By Thine own eternal Spirit
Rule in all our hearts alone;
By Thine all sufficient merit,
Raise us to Thy glorious throne.

— Charles Wesley, 1744

The hauntingly beautiful carol *O Come, O Come, Emmanuel* contains an amazing collection of spiritual truths that represent the experiences and expressions of people from various backgrounds, cultures, and periods of history. Originating in the medieval Roman Catholic Church of the twelfth century, this carol contains a series of seven antiphons, or short statements, sung at the beginning of prayers during the Advent season. Each of these statements greets the Savior with one of the many titles ascribed to him in the Scriptures, such as Emmanuel, Day-spring, and Desire of nations. (Only three of the seven appear here.)

The modal melody of *Emmanuel* was originally a plainsong, or chant, the earliest form of singing in the church.

During the nineteenth century, a number of Anglican ministers rediscovered many ancient Greek and Latin hymns and translated them into English. One of the ministers was John M. Neale. His translation of this Latin Advent prayer compares God's people, separated from heaven, with Israel separated from God's holy temple in Jerusalem during their Babylonian exile.

As one of the carols sung early in the Christmas season, *O Come, O Come, Emmanuel* emphasizes the anticipation of the ancient Israelites, prayerfully expecting the Messiah to come to earth and "ransom captive Israel." Tragically, the Messiah did come unto his own people to establish a spiritual kingdom, but his people did not receive him. The prayer of this Advent carol is that we would not miss his coming but instead receive him as our Emmanuel—our "God with us."

O Come, O Come, Emmanuel

O come, O come, Emmanuel
And ransom captive Israel,
That mourns in lonely exile here
Until the Son of God appear.
Rejoice! Rejoice! Emmanuel
Shall come to thee, O Israel!

O come, Thou Dayspring, come and cheer
Our spirits by Thine advent here;
And drive away the shades of night,
And pierce the clouds and bring us light!
Rejoice! Rejoice! Emmanuel
Shall come to thee, O Israel!

O come, Desire of nations, bind
All peoples in one heart and mind;
Bid envy, strife and quarrels cease;
Fill all the world with heaven's peace.
Rejoice! Rejoice! Emmanuel
Shall come to thee, O Israel!

— Latin hymn,
Psalteriolum Cantionum Catholicarum, A.D. 1210;
translation by John M. Neale;
last verse by Henry S. Coffin

"And when the days are fulfilled
    and you shall sleep
    with your fathers;
I will set up your seed after you,
    which shall proceed
    out of your bowels,
And I will establish
    his kingdom.

"He shall build a house
    for my name,
And I will establish the throne
    of his kingdom for ever.

"I will be his father
    and he shall be my son.
And your house and your kingdom
    shall be established for ever
    before you.
Your throne shall be established
    forever."

By the prophet Nathan to King David, c. 1000 B.C.
2 SAMUEL 7:12-16

"He shall build me a house,
    and I will establish his throne forever.

"I will be his father,
    and he shall be my son:
And I will not remove
    my mercy from him,
    as I removed it from those
    that were before.

"But I will establish him
    in my house
    and in my kingdom forever:
And his throne shall be established
    for evermore."

By the prophet Nathan to King David, c. 1000 B.C.
1 CHRONICLES 17:11-14

Many hymns and carols that placed an emphasis on Mary were summarily dismissed or sometimes removed from public worship by the Lutheran reformers of the sixteenth century. This fifteenth century traditional German folk carol survived those repressionist times primarily because its message can be allegorically attributed to Christ.

Harmonized in 1609 by Michael Praetorius and translated in 1894 by Theodore Baker, this exquisite carol weaves a lovely meditation about the Rose of Sharon (Song of Songs 2:1) and the stem of Jesse (Isaiah 11:1). These beautiful portrayals of Jesus, the incarnate son of God, were meaningful symbols for many of the German people who tenderly cared for their flowering rose trees.

The lyrics' repetition of "half-spent was the night" intimates that Christ's birth almost went unnoticed amid the bustle of the Roman taxation in Bethlehem. *Lo! How a Rose E'er Blooming* reminds us to remember Christ's birth amid our own busy schedules during the Christmas season.

Lo! How a Rose E'er Blooming

Lo, how a Rose e'er blooming
From tender stem hath sprung!
Of Jesse's lineage coming
As men of old have sung.
It came a Flow'ret bright,
Amid the cold of winter
When half-spent was the night.

Isaiah 'twas foretold it,
The Rose I have in mind;
With Mary we behold it,
The virgin mother kind.
To show God's love aright
She bore to men a Savior
When half-spent was the night.

— 15th-century German carol;
translation by Theodore Baker

As Joseph Was A-Walking

As Joseph was a-walking
He heard an angel sing,
"This night shall be the birth time
Of Christ, the heav'nly King."

"He neither shall be born
In housen nor in hall,
Nor in the place of Paradise,
But in an ox's stall."

"He neither shall be clothed
In purple nor in pall,
But in the fair white linen
As wear sweet babies all."

As Joseph was a-walking
Thus did the angel sing;
And Mary's Child at midnight
Was born to be our King.

— Author unknown

THE ANNOUNCEMENT TO JOSEPH

MARY HAD PROMISED to become Joseph's wife. In fact, they were engaged.

But before they were married, before they lived together, Joseph learned that Mary was pregnant (by the Holy Spirit). Being a man of principle, and at the same time not wanting her to be publicly disgraced, Joseph resolved to discreetly break off their engagement.

While Joseph was tossing in bed one night, contemplating the best course to follow, an angel of the Lord appeared to him in a dream.

"Joseph, son of David," the angel said, "do not be afraid to make Mary your wife. The baby in her was conceived by the Holy Spirit of God. It is a boy! A son! You are to name him Jesus (which means Savior), because it is he who will save his people from their sins."

All of this occurred fulfilling a prediction that the Lord God made through the prophet Isaiah, hundreds of years earlier:

> **"Behold, a virgin shall be with child and shall bear a son,**
> **and they shall call his name Immanuel."**
> (Immanuel translated means *God with us.*)

So when Joseph awoke from his sleep, he did exactly as the angel of the Lord commanded him. He took Mary as his wife. But he did not sleep with her until after she gave birth to her first son.

And he named the baby Jesus.

MATTHEW 1:18-25

Christmas Gift

Shout! Shout this Christmas wish
Around the world a ringing
Peace! Peace to all the earth!
"Let's send the message winging!"

Raise! Raise your voices high
In praise and adoration;
Christ came with peace and hope
For ev'ry man and nation.

— Author unknown

ELIZABETH'S SONG

AT A TIME early in her pregnancy, Mary got her things together and hurried away to the hill country, to a town in Judea. There she went to the home of Zacharias, and greeted her cousin Elizabeth.

At the instant Mary greeted her, Elizabeth felt her unborn baby virtually leap within her, and she herself was filled with the Holy Spirit.

Elizabeth cried out:

> "Oh, Mary, how marvelously God
>   has blessed you!
>   singling you out
>   from all the women in the world!
> And how specially blessed is the child
>   who will come from your womb!
> What an honor it is for me
>   to have the mother of my Lord
>   visit my home!
> For the instant you greeted me
>   my baby leaped for joy within me!
> How specially blessed is the woman
>   who trusts God
>   to keep his promise to her!"

LUKE 1:39-45

MARY'S SONG

MARY RESPONDED with an outburst of thanksgiving:

"All that is within me praises the Lord,
    and my spirit delights in God, my Savior;
For he has seen fit to notice me,
    his most humble servant, a nobody!
    For from now on, forever
    throughout all generations,
    the world will regard me
    as the woman God favored,
    because Almighty God
    has done great things for me.
Holy is his name!
He is merciful
    to generation after generation,
    to those who reverence him.
How powerful and strong is his arm!
How he routs the proud and the haughty!
How he disposes strong rulers
    and elevates the ordinary!
The hungry he has filled with good things,
    but the rich go away with empty hands.
And now he has come to help his servant Israel.

His promise of mercy has not been forgotten,
    the promises he made to our ancestors,
to Abraham and all his descendants,
    forever and forever."

Mary stayed with Elizabeth about three months and then returned to her own home.

LUKE 1:46-56

Isaac Watts wrote some 600 hymns throughout his life, among them *Joy to the World!* This carol was first published in 1719. Watts himself entitled the song *The Messiah's Coming and Kingdom*, and it is a paraphrase of verses taken from the latter half of Psalm 98. In these verses the psalmist calls on all of creation, man and nature alike, to celebrate the singing of a new song of joy before the Lord.

George Frederic Handel, best known for his 1741 composition *The Messiah*, was a contemporary and colleague of Isaac Watts. He is credited with being the source of this carol's melody. In 1936, an American choir director, Lowell Mason, rearranged a portion of Handel's *Messiah* to fit the words of Watts' paraphrase from Psalm 98. Thus, almost a century after Watts wrote his poem, a favorite Christmas carol was born.

Although several other music compositions have been sung to Isaac Watts' famous words, it is largely through the combined talents of an eighteenth-century English poet, a cosmopolitan German musical giant, and a nineteenth-century American choir director that we can collectively proclaim the true joy of Advent when we sing this beloved carol today.

Joy to the World!

Joy to the world! the Lord is come!
Let earth receive her King;
Let ev'ry heart prepare Him room,
And heav'n and nature sing,
And heav'n and nature sing,
And heav'n and heav'n and nature sing.

No more let sins and sorrows grow,
Nor thorns infest the ground;
He comes to make his blessings flow
Far as the curse is found,
Far as the curse is found,
Far as, far as the curse is found.

He rules the world with truth and grace.
And makes the nations prove
The glories of His righteousness.
And wonders of His love,
And wonders of His love,
And wonders and wonders of His love.

— Isaac Watts; based on Psalm 98

"Behold,
    I will send my messenger
    and he shall prepare
    the way before me:
And the Lord whom you seek
    shall suddenly come
    to his temple,
    even the messenger
    of the covenant,
    in whom you delight:
Behold, he shall come,"
    says the Lord of Hosts.

By the prophet Malachi, c. 430 B.C.
MALACHI 3:1

The people that walked in darkness
    have seen a great light:
They dwell in the land
    of the shadow of death,
Upon them has
    the light shone.

By the prophet Isaiah, c.700 B.C.
ISAIAH 9:2

THE BIRTH OF JOHN

WHEN IT WAS TIME for Elizabeth to have her baby, she gave birth to a son. Her neighbors and relatives heard of the great goodness the Lord had shown her and rejoiced and celebrated with her.

When the baby was eight days old, they took him to the temple to have him circumcised. Everyone assumed that the child would be named Zacharias after his father. But Elizabeth said, "No, he must be named John."

"But none of your relatives is called John," they retorted. Then they turned to his father Zacharias, and, by making signs, they asked him what name he wanted. He gestured for a writing tablet and wrote, "His name is John." They were all astonished!

Immediately Zacharias' ability to speak returned, his voice was restored, and he began shouting praises to God!

Fear struck all of their neighbors as the news of all these incidents spread about the hill country of Judea. It made a deep impression on everyone who heard about it, and they asked themselves, "What kind of special person will he become?" For the hand of the Lord was plainly on him.

Filled with the Holy Spirit, his father Zacharias prophesied:

> "Praise the Lord, the God of Israel!
> He has visited his people
>   and brought redemption.
> He has raised up a mighty Savior for us
>   in the house of his servant David.
> It is exactly as the prophets predicted,
>   that we should be saved
>   from our enemies,
>   and from the hand of all who hate us;

To show us the mercy
    promised to our fathers,
And to remember his holy covenants,
    the oath he swore to our father Abraham;
To grant us that we,
    being freed from the hand of our enemies,
    might serve him without fear
    in holiness and righteousness before him
    all the days of our lives.
And you, child, will be called
    'The prophet of the Most High'
    For you will go before the Lord,
    preparing the way for him, giving his people
    the knowledge of salvation,
    through the forgiveness of their sins,
    because of the loving compassion of God.
Heaven's dawn is about to break
    shining light on those in darkness,
    those who are now
    beneath the shadow of death,
    guiding our feet in the path of peace."

The child grew and became spiritually strong. When he grew up, he left home and lived in the wilderness country until the time came to begin his public ministry in Israel.

LUKE 1:57-80

This joyful call to proclaim the Messiah's birth was created in the late nineteenth century or very early twentieth century. The original refrain was a composition by Frederick J. Work, a black, Nashville-born composer and choir director at Fisk University. Work's son, John Wesley Work, was also a professor at Fisk. Familiar with the original refrain, and appreciating its message, the younger Work shaped and harmonized the melody, added some original stanzas, and published the entire carol in 1907 in a small booklet entitled *Folk Songs of the American Negro*.

Two other familiar spirituals contained in the booklet were *Somebody's Knockin' at Your Door* and *Were You There?*

During the early part of the 1900s, each Christmas morning at five o'clock, the Fisk Jubilee Singers strolled the campus of Fisk University singing Christmas carols. Students and townspeople alike recalled these exuberant times, with everyone agreeing that their favorite carol was **Go, Tell It on the Mountain!**

The words of this black spiritual echo the prophecy of Isaiah 40:9. The prophet's call to "go up on a high mountain" to "bring good tidings to Zion" finds a joyful voice in this uncomplicated carol, as it reminds us to share good tidings of peace and Christ's gift of eternal life with others at Christmastime.

Go, Tell It on the Mountain

While shepherds kept their watching
O'er silent flocks by night,
Behold! throughout the heavens
There shone a holy light.

The shepherds feared and trembled
When lo! above the earth
Rang out the angel chorus
That hailed our Savior's birth.

Down in a lowly manger
The humble Christ was born,
And brought us God's salvation
That blessed Christmas morn.

Go, tell it on the mountain,
Over the hills and everywhere;
Go, tell it on the mountain
That Jesus Christ is born!

— John W. Work, Jr.

"I the Lord have called you
in righteousness,
    and will hold your hand,
    and will keep you,
    and give you a covenant of the people,
    for a light to the Gentiles."

"I bring near my righteousness;
    it shall not be far off,
And my salvation shall not tarry:
And I will place salvation in Zion
    For Israel my glory."

"It is a light thing
    that you should be my servant
    to raise up the tribe of Jacob,
    and to restore the preserved of Israel:
I will also give you a light to the Gentiles,
    that you may be my salvation
    unto the end of the earth."

By the prophet Isaiah, c. 700 B.C.
ISAIAH 42:6; 46:13; 49:6

THE BIRTH OF JESUS

Jesus' birth

The proclamation by the angels

The visit by the shepherds

The temple visit

The testimony of Simeon

The testimony of Anna

The visit by the Magi

The escape to Egypt

ohn Byrom was an accomplished English poet. Though Byrom had several children, his favorite was his daughter Dolly. As Christmas 1745 neared, Dolly asked for a special Christmas gift. Byrom promised to write her a poem for Christmas. It would be written especially for her, and for no one else.

Every day Dolly reminded her father of his promise to her. And on Christmas morning, when she ran down to breakfast, Dolly found several presents waiting for her. One of Dolly's presents was an envelope that was addressed to her in her father's handwriting. It was the first gift she opened on that Christmas day. To her great delight, she found a poem entitled "Christmas Day for Dolly." Dolly's Christmas gift was later published in the *Manchester Mercury* under the title "Christians Awake."

With its straightforward retelling of the Christmas story, *Christians, Awake!* proclaims the message that one day we will join the angels as they stand by Christ's throne. Together we will sing "eternal praise to heaven's Almighty King." Every glorious day will be Christmas!

Christians, Awake!

Christians, awake! salute the happy morn
Whereon the Savior of the world was born;
Rise to adore the mystery of love,
Which hosts of angels chanted from above;
With them the joyful tidings first begun
Of God Incarnate and the Virgin's Son.

Then to the watchful shepherds it was told,
Who heard the angelic herald's voice, "Behold,
I bring good tidings of a Savior's birth
To you and all the nations upon earth;
This day hath God fulfilled His promised word;
This day is born a Savior, Christ the Lord."

Then may we hope, the angelic hosts among,
To sing, redeemed, a glad triumphal song;
He that was born upon this joyful day
Around us all His glory shall display;
Saved by His love, incessant we shall sing
Eternal praise to heaven's Almighty King.

— John Byrom, 1745

Who Is He in Yonder Stall?

Who is He in yonder stall,
At whose feet the shepherds fall?
'Tis the Lord! Oh, wondrous story!
'Tis the Lord, the King of glory.
Jesus Savior!

Who is He in yonder cot,
Bending to His toilsome lot?
'Tis the Lord, the King of glory!
At His feet we humbly fall.
'Tis the Lord, we crown Him
Lord of all.

— Benjamin R. Hanby, 1857

JESUS' BIRTH

IN THOSE DAYS, toward the end of Mary's pregnancy, the Emperor Caesar Augustus decreed that a census be taken of the entire Roman Empire. This was the first census taken when Quirinius was governor of Syria. Everyone was required to register in his own city.

Since Joseph was a descendant of David, he went up from the city of Nazareth in Galilee, to Bethlehem, the city of David, in Judea. Mary, who was engaged to him and by now was close to full term, accompanied him, for she, too, was of the house of David and had to register.

While they were there, Mary went into labor and gave birth to her first-born son. She wrapped him in swaddling clothes and, because there had been no room for them in the inn, she gently laid him in a manger.

LUKE 2:1-7

Still, Still, Still

Still, still, still,
He sleeps this night so chill!
The Virgin's tender arms enfolding,
Warm and safe the Child are holding.
Still, still, still,
He sleeps this night so chill!

Sleeps, sleeps, sleeps,
While we Thy vigil keep.
And angels, from heaven singing,
Songs of jubilation bringing.
Sleeps, sleeps, sleeps,
While we Thy vigil keep.

— Author unknown;
18th-century Austrian folk carol

Infant Holy, Infant Lowly

Infant holy, Infant lowly,
For His bed a cattle stall;
Oxen lowing, little knowing
Christ, the Babe, is Lord of all.
Swift are winging, angels singing,
Noels ringing, tidings bringing:
Christ, the Babe, is Lord of all!
Christ, the Babe, is Lord of all!

Flocks were sleeping; shepherds keeping
Vigil till the morning new
Saw the glory, heard the story
Tidings of a gospel true.
Thus rejoicing, free from sorrow,
Praises voicing greet the morrow:
Christ, the Babe, was born for you!
Christ, the Babe, was born for you!

— Polish carol;
paraphrase by Edith M. G. Reed, 1925

This English translation of a Polish carol first appeared in print in 1925 in *Music and Youth*, edited and published by Edith Reed.

The tune had been sung in England half a century earlier, but the text had never before appeared in print.

The title originally attributed to it by Edith Reed was *W. Zlobia Lezy*, Polish for **He Lies in the Cradle.** In preparing the 1951 Hymnal for Congregational Singing, the Polish title, until it was subsequently corrected, was mistakenly confused as the name of the Polish author, W. Zlobia Lezy.

Part of the charm of this child's carol is its nursery-rhyme appeal, giving the accumulative cascading effect of the rhyming sounds themselves—winging, singing, ringing, bringing us to Christ, the babe who is Lord of all.

He Lies in the Cradle

Infant holy,
Infant lowly,
For his bed a cattle stall,
Oxen lowing,
Little knowing
Christ the babe is Lord of all.
Swift are winging
Angels singing,
Noels ringing,
Tidings bringing:
Christ the babe is Lord of all.

— 19th-century Polish folk carol

Though this carol is often ascribed to Martin Luther, the German reformer was not its creator. Several hymnbooks also incorrectly credit the carol's music to a Carl Mueller. In fact, the carol was virtually unknown in Germany until early in 1900.

Instead, an anonymous composer published *Away in a Manger* in Philadelphia in 1885. Two years later, in 1887, American James Ramsey Murray composed the most popular melody for this carol. However, Jonathan E. Spilman's 1838 melody, which was originally intended for the folk ballad *Flow Gently Sweet Afton*, is also often paired with *Away in a Manger.*

In the early 1940s, American musician Richard S. Hill probed for the carol's origin and correctly credited Murray for his popular musical score. Regardless of its origins, *Away in a Manger* softly captures the wonder of the birth of Jesus in a tender lullaby that returns all who sing it to the peace of childhood once again.

Away in a Manger

Away in a manger, no crib for a bed,
The little Lord Jesus laid down his sweet head;
The stars in the sky look'd down where he lay,
The little Lord Jesus, asleep on the hay.

The cattle are lowing, the poor Baby wakes,
But little Lord Jesus, no crying he makes;
I love thee, Lord Jesus! look down from the sky,
And stay by my cradle till morning is nigh.

Be near me, Lord Jesus; I ask Thee to stay
Close by me forever, and love me, I pray.
Bless all the dear children in Thy tender care,
And fit us for heaven, to live with Thee there.

— Author unknown

*M*ary Macdougall Macdonald composed numerous Scottish Gaelic songs and hymns of genuine beauty. One was this Gaelic carol, *The Child of Agh*, meaning "child of happiness, power or wonder."

Mary Macdougall was born in 1789 on the Isle of Mull, one of the Inner Hebrides islands. Her father and brother were Baptist ministers. Her husband, Neill Macdonald, worked their small plot of land, which he supplemented by fishing.

Mary Macdougall Macdonald died on the Isle of Mull at the age of eighty-three.

Leon Macbear, an authority on Scottish Gaelic language and literature, translated *The Child of Agh* into English as **Child in a Manger**, retaining its original Gaelic tune. He included it in his *Songs and Hymns of the Gall*, first published in Edinburgh in 1888.

Child in a Manger

Child in a manger,
Infant of Mary;
Outcast and stranger,
Lord of all;
Child who inherits
All our transgressions,
All our demerits
On him fall.

— Mary Macdougall Macdonald

On Christmas Eve in 1818, at the church of St. Nicholas in Oberndorf, Austria, the pipe organ would not play. The mice had chewed through the organ's bellows and made several nests inside the pipes themselves. Father Joseph Mohr quickly penned a new song to substitute for the one that was scheduled to be played on the organ that evening. Franz Gruber, the church organist and village schoolmaster, wrote the now famous music. At that Christmas Eve service, the two men sang *Silent Night* as a duet, with Franz Gruber providing accompaniment on guitar.

That would have been the end of the story if not for the organ repairman. Karl Mauracher traveled to Oberndorf to repair the instrument. Upon hearing the story of the Christmas Eve service, the repairman asked for a copy of the new song. He subsequently shared it with other organists and churches throughout upper Austria. Thirteen years later, *Silent Night* was sung at the Leipzig Fair, and it was finally published in 1838, twenty years after its composition and first performance. German immigrants brought the carol to America, where it was translated into English in several different versions. The most familiar English translation was the work of an Episcopal minister, John Freeman Young, who in 1863 first published the carol we sing today.

Though some may say it was coincidence, others contend that God's hand brought us this beloved carol. Father Mohr served in the Oberndorf church for only a short time, and Franz Gruber was supposed to have attended another church that evening. But whether through mishap or divine intervention, a simple song left a tiny town in the Austrian Alps and traveled the globe to become the best-loved carol of Christmas.

Silent Night

Silent night! Holy night!
All is calm, all is bright
Round yon Virgin Mother and Child!
Holy Infant, so tender and mild,
Sleep in heavenly peace.
Sleep in heavenly peace.

Silent night! Holy night!
Shepherds quake at the sight,
Glories stream from heaven afar,
Heav'nly hosts sing Alleluia;
Christ, the Savior is born!
Christ, the Savior is born!

Silent night! Holy night!
Son of God, love's pure light,
Radiant beams from Thy holy face,
With the dawn of redeeming grace,
Jesus, Lord at Thy birth!
Jesus, Lord at Thy birth.

— Joseph Mohr

During the early 1860s, Philadelphia clergyman Phillips Brooks visited the Holy Land. Several years later, in a reflective mood, Brooks penned a brief poem that recalled some of the sights he had seen.

He showed his composition to Lewis Redner, a real estate agent and part-time organist for Brooks's church. Redner had been struggling to put together the final pieces for an upcoming Sunday School Christmas program.

With Brooks's poem in mind, Redner slept the night before the program with a deep assurance that all would be well. At the first light of dawn, Redner awoke with a melody sounding in his head. He jotted the notes down as quickly as he could and hurried to play the piece for Reverend Brooks.

When the men matched Redner's melody with the words of Brooks's poem, the two fit together perfectly. Because a pastor and a part-time organist had been willing instruments in God's orchestration, the beautiful carol *O Little Town of Bethlehem* was born.

O Little Town of Bethlehem

O little town of Bethlehem,
How still we see thee lie;
Above thy deep and dreamless sleep
The silent stars go by:
Yet in thy dark streets shineth
The everlasting Light;
The hopes and fears of all the years
Are met in thee tonight.

For Christ is born of Mary;
And gathered all above,
While mortals sleep, the angels keep
Their watch of wond'ring love,
O morning stars, together
Proclaim the holy birth;
And praises sing to God the King
And peace to men on earth.

— Phillips Brooks

Though Louis Benson graduated from law school at the University of Pennsylvania, he practiced law for just seven years. In 1877, Benson made a career change and entered Princeton Theological Seminary. Because he was very interested in hymns and songs of worship, Benson's library of hymns eventually grew to 9000 volumes.

Upon his graduation from Princeton, Benson was ordained and became the pastor of a church in Germantown, Pennsylvania. While pastoring this congregation, Benson penned the lyrics for *O Sing a Song of Bethlehem*, but the poem remained unpublished for several years.

It wasn't until Louis Benson met Ralph Vaughan Williams that *O Sing a Song of Bethlehem* was finally completed. Benson and Williams shared a love for hymns. Many hymn tunes can be traced back to Vaughan Williams, one of the best-known English composers of the twentieth century. In 1889, Benson and Vaughan Williams's collaboration produced this carol, weaving the gospel message with a touching English folk tune. As we sing these words at Christmastime, we can rejoice at the coming of the Christ child and at the news of peace on earth.

O Sing a Song of Bethlehem

O sing a song of Bethlehem,
of shepherds watching there,
And of the news that came to them
from angels in the air.
The light that shone on Bethlehem
fills all the world today;
Of Jesus' birth and peace on earth
the angels sing alway.

O sing a song of Nazareth,
of sunny days of joy;
O sing of fragrant flowers' breath,
and of the sinless Boy.
For now the flowers of Nazareth
in every heart may grow;
Now spreads the fame of His dear Name
on all the winds that blow.

— Louis F. Benson, 1889

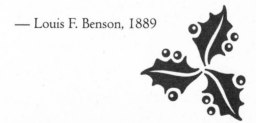

*L*egend says that in the mid-fourteenth century, German mystic Heinrich Suso wrote the words to this carol after dancing and singing with the angels. Bartholomaeus Gesius adapted Suso's composition in 1601 and called it *In Dulci Jubilo*, which means *With Sweet Shouting*. Later Johann Sebastian Bach arranged it for the organ, and later still John Stainer wrote a choral version of this ancient Latin hymn.

John Mason Neale, an Anglican priest who wrote or translated more than 700 hymns, had a hand in bringing this carol to the English language. Because many of his views went against the Anglican hierarchy of the day, Neale was never assigned his own parish but instead worked as a warden in an almshouse. It was there in 1853 that he paraphrased this medieval song from Latin into English, then published it as a new carol, **Good Christian Men, Rejoice**, in his songbook entitled *Carols for Christmastide*.

This wonderfully joyous carol still retains its ancient fourteenth-century German flavor and melody. Now, with heart and soul and voice, we can join with celebrants throughout the centuries in rejoicing that Jesus Christ is born today!

Good Christian Men, Rejoice

Good Christian men, rejoice
With heart and soul and voice,
Give ye heed to what we say:
News! News! Jesus Christ is born today!
Ox and ass, before Him bow,
And He is in the manger now;
Christ is born today! Christ is born today.

Good Christian men, rejoice
With heart and soul and voice,
Now ye need not fear the grave:
Peace! Peace! Jesus Christ was born to save.
Calls you one and calls you all,
To gain His everlasting hall;
Christ was born to save, Christ was born to save.

— Heinrich Suso

The Birthday of a King

In the little village of Bethlehem,
There lay a Child one day;
And the sky was bright
With a holy light
O'er the place where Jesus lay.

'Twas a humble birthplace, but, oh, how much
God gave to us that day,
From the manger bed
What a path has led,
What a perfect, holy way.

Alleluia! O how the angels sang!
Alleluia! How it rang!
And the sky was bright
With a holy light
'Twas the birthday of a King.

—William H. Neidlinger, 1894

THE PROCLAMATION BY THE ANGELS

IN THE FIELDS outside of Bethlehem that night, some shepherds were tending their sheep. Suddenly an angel of the Lord appeared in their midst, and the glory of the Lord shone radiantly. The whole field lit up with his presence. The shepherds were petrified!

"Stop being afraid," the angel said. "I have come to bring you good news which will bring great joy to all people of the world. The Messiah has come! Your Savior was born today in Bethlehem, the town of David! You will know you have found him when you discover a baby wrapped in swaddling clothes, lying in a manger."

Suddenly, an army of heavenly hosts appeared with the angel, filling the sky. They raised their voices in song:

"Glory to God in highest heaven!
And on earth, peace to those
    with whom God is pleased!"

Then, as quickly as they appeared, the angels were gone back into heaven.

LUKE 2:8-14

The background of this splendid carol and its most common English translation is uncertain. An early rendition is documented in an 1855 French collection of Christmas songs. Soon after, the verses were translated into English and appeared in England in an 1862 hymnbook. Though *Angels We Have Heard on High* retains its French melody, the carol did not take its familiar form until it was published in a 1916 American carol collection.

The Latin phrase in this hymn, *Gloria in excelsis Deo*, echoes the message that the angels brought to the shepherds on that hillside outside Bethlehem so long ago. As we sing this song at Christmastime, we also join in bringing "glory to God in the highest."

Angels We Have Heard on High

Angels we have heard on high,
Sweetly singing o'er the plains,
And the mountains in reply,
Echoing their joyous strains.
Gloria in excelsis Deo, Gloria in excelsis Deo.

Shepherds, why this jubilee?
Why your joyous strains prolong?
What the gladsome tidings be
Which inspire your heav'nly song?
Gloria in excelsis Deo, Gloria in excelsis Deo.

Come to Bethlehem, and see
Him whose birth the angels sing:
Come, adore on bended knee,
Christ the Lord, the newborn King.
Gloria in excels is Deo, Gloria in excelsis Deo.

— Author unknown

*M*ore than 6,500 hymns flowed from the pen of Charles Wesley. *Hark! The Herald Angels Sing* is one of his two most popular songs, and one of the top four favorite Christmas carols of all time. Written just one year after Wesley's spiritual renewal in 1738, this carol reflects both the joy and the theological basis of Wesley's new relationship with God. The carol resounds with a dominant theme: God and sinful people are reconciled.

Wesley's text has been blended with a melody written by the master composer of the early nineteenth century, Felix Mendelssohn. A prolific composer, in 1840 Mendelssohn wrote a festive chorale for men's voices and brass instruments. The melody was aptly named *Mendelssohn.* Fifteen years later, English musician William H. Cummings became enchanted with the melody and adapted it to Wesley's *Hark! The Herald Angels* lyrics. This adaptation was first published in the *Congregational Hymn and Tune Book* in 1857.

Ironically, John Wesley and Felix Mendelssohn died before their two creations were joined to form this Christmas carol. But their musical message reminds us at Christmas that Christ was born so that we can become children of God. For this, and so much more, we can sing with the angels, "Glory to the newborn King!"

Hark! The Herald Angels Sing

Hark! The herald angels sing,
"Glory to the newborn King!
Peace on earth, and mercy mild;
God and sinners reconciled!"
Joyful, all ye nations rise;
Join the triumph of the skies;
With th' angelic hosts proclaim,
"Christ is born in Bethlehem!"
Hark! The herald angels sing,
"Glory to the newborn King."

Hail the heav'n-born Prince of Peace!
Hail the Sun of Righteousness!
Light and life to all he brings,
Ris'n with healing in his wings.
Mild he lays his glory by,
Born that man no more may die,
Born to raise the sons of Earth,
Born to give them second birth.
Hark! The herald angels sing,
"Glory to the newborn King."

— Charles Wesley, 1739

English hymn writer and journalist James Montgomery created the lyrics to this great carol in 1816, basing them on the eighteenth-century French carol *Angels We Have Heard on High*. The son of Moravian missionaries, Montgomery became a communicant of the Anglican church and composed more than 360 hymns in his lifetime. *Angels From the Realms of Glory* was written for inclusion in Montgomery's Christmas Eve column in *The Iris*, a small newspaper that Montgomery edited.

Fifty years after the poem was written, Henry Smart composed a piece of music to accompany the verses. Smart had lost his sight in 1865, so his composition of the 1867 melody originated completely in his heart and memory. The tune was named *Regent Square* after the name of the Presbyterian church in London, where it was written.

The central focus of this carol is the adoration of the newborn Messiah from the perspective of those who witnessed the nativity firsthand, moving from the angels to the shepherds and finally to the wise men. Yet whether angels from heaven or mortals on earth, Montgomery's words call us all to recognize that the child in the manger is God's royalty: "Christ, the newborn King."

Angels From the Realms of Glory

Angels from the realms of glory,
Wing your flight o'er all the earth;
Ye who sang creation's story,
Now proclaim Messiah's birth:
Come and worship, Come and worship,
Worship Christ the newborn King.

Shepherds in the fields abiding,
Watching o'er your flocks by night,
God with man is now residing,
Yonder shines the infant Light:
Come and worship, Come and worship,
Worship Christ the newborn King.

Sages, leave your contemplations,
Brighter visions beam afar;
Seek the great Desire of nations,
Ye have seen his natal star:
Come and worship, Come and worship,
Worship Christ the newborn King.

— James Montgomery, 1816

Of all of the German Christmas carols, only *O Christmas Tree* is better known than **From Heaven Above to Earth I Come**, which the great reformer Martin Luther wrote for the Christmas of 1535. The song was sung at the annual Christmas Eve festival held at the Luther home. History says that Luther wrote this hymn especially for his five-year-old son Hans to help him understand and celebrate the coming of the Christ child.

A man dressed as an angel would sing the opening verses, and the children would respond with the last verse, "Welcome to earth, thou noble guest." Four years later, Luther composed the now famous melody, and in 1734 Bach adapted this great chorale for his *Christmas Oratorio*.

From Heaven Above to Earth I Come has been called "the carol of the Reformation." Its retelling of Christ's birth from an angel's perspective reminds us that the announcement by the angel was the greatest news of that first Christmas, and every Christmas thereafter. The Christ of Christmas is still the "joy of all the earth."

From Heaven Above to Earth I Come

From heaven above to earth I come
To bear good news to every home;
Glad tidings of great joy I bring,
Whereof I now will say and sing:

To you this night is born a child
Of Mary, chosen mother mild;
This little child, of lowly birth,
Shall be the joy of all the earth.

Glory to God in highest heav'n
Who unto man his Son hath giv'n.
While angels sing with tender mirth,
A glad new year to all the earth.

Welcome to earth, thou noble guest,
Through whom e'en wicked men are blest!
Thou comest to share our misery;
What can we render, Lord, to thee?

— Martin Luther, 1531

Massachusetts minister Edmund Hamilton Sears created this classic carol of optimism one winter's night in December 1849. Although Sears graduated from Harvard as a Unitarian, he believed and preached the divinity of Christ.

Sears authored a number of books but wrote only two published hymns, each intended for the Christmas season. His lesser known *Calm on the Listening Ear* was written while he was a divinity student at Harvard. Fifteen years later he penned **It Came Upon the Midnight Clear.** Since its publication in 1849, scarcely a hymnal has been printed which does not include this Christmas favorite, one of the first carols written by an American.

Richard Willis, a contemporary of Edmund Sears and a close friend of Felix Mendelssohn, composed the excellent, flowing melody in 1850. Paired with Sears's lyrics, this carol assures us that this "weary world" with its "sad and lowly plains" can find God's peace by receiving his grace. The angels' announcement of "peace on earth" has been revealed in Christ—the Prince of Peace.

It Came Upon the Midnight Clear

It came upon the midnight clear,
That glorious song of old,
From angels bending near the earth
To touch their harps of gold;
"Peace on the earth, good will to men,
From heav'ns all gracious King."
The world in solemn stillness lay
To hear the angels sing.

For, lo, the days are hastening on,
By prophets seen of old,
When, with the ever-circling years,
Shall come the time foretold,
When the new heaven and earth shall own
The Prince of Peace their King,
And the whole world send back the song
Which now the angels sing.

— Edmund H. Sears, 1849

Despite the repeated use of the word *Noel* in this Christmas carol, this song is not French but is one of Great Britain's most popular carols. Written in the sixteenth century in a remote Southwest region of Cornwall, the words to this joyous carol were first published in a collection of carols in 1823. The music was published a decade later, and since then, its form has remained basically unchanged for almost two centuries.

However, *The First Noel* is one of only a very few Christmas carols that includes a factual error. The second stanza incorrectly ascribes to the shepherds the first sighting of the star, a rare mistake among all our Christmas carols which so clearly and correctly present the true story of Christmas and the pure message of deliverance from sin, and salvation through that child born in a stable over 2,000 years ago.

The word *noel* originated as an expression of joy, originally shouted or sung (or both) to commemorate the birth of Jesus.

Today, two centuries after its composition, we still raise our voices together in singing *The First Noel*. As we, in one accord, celebrate Christmas, we remember that at its center, Christmas is a celebration of joy and gladness. God came to earth as a small baby, born in a manger—a baby, born to be our King.

The First Noel

The first Noel the angels did say
Was to certain poor shepherds in fields as they lay;
In fields where they lay keeping their sheep,
On a cold winter's night that was so deep.

They looked up and saw a Star
Bright in the East beyond them far.
And to the earth it gave great light,
And so it continued both day and night.

This star drew nigh to the northwest,
O'er Bethlehem it took its rest,
And there it did both stop and stay,
Right over the place where Jesus lay.

Then let us all with one accord
Sing praises to our heavenly Lord,
That hath made heav'n and earth of naught,
And with his blood mankind hath bought.

Noel, Noel, Noel, Noel,
Born is the King of Israel.

— Author unknown

Josiah Holland, who wrote this carol, gave up a brief career as a medical doctor to pursue publishing. Eventually he became a founder of *Scribners' Magazine* and served as its editor until his death in 1881.

There's a Song in the Air reflects Holland's keen imagination and his sense of lyrical beauty. The song of angels and the star of the east are the two pegs on which this familiar carol is hung.

Each stanza concludes with a tribute to the kingship of Jesus. The fourth stanza concludes as a doxology of praise for the salvation that Jesus brings—which comes down through the night of our own darkness to give us light and hope.

There's a Song in the Air

There's a song in the air!
There's a star in the sky!
There's a mother's deep prayer
And a baby's low cry!
And the star rains its fire while the beautiful sing.
For the manger of Bethlehem cradles a King!

There's a tumult of joy
O'er the wonderful birth,
For the Virgin's sweet Boy
Is the Lord of the earth.
And the star rains its fire while the beautiful sing.
For the manger of Bethlehem cradles a King!

We rejoice in the light,
And we echo the song
That comes down through the night
From the heavenly throng,
And we shout to the lovely evangel they bring,
And we greet in His cradle our Savior and King!

— Josiah G. Holland, 1874

orn in 1607, Johann Rist showed an interest in hymn writing while still in college. After graduation, Rist tutored children in Hamburg, Germany, continuing his studies in Hebrew, mathematics, and medicine in the university there. But Rist contracted a severe illness and was forced to give up tutoring. While he recuperated, Rist met a woman named Elizabeth Stapfel. The two married and spent the remainder of their lives in Hamburg. Emperor Ferdinand II named Rist his poet laureate in 1644, and in 1653 he raised Rist to the nobility.

Rist's wife became friends with the court musicians. Johann Schop was the leader of the municipal musicians' group in Hamburg. He was a well-known violinist in addition to being an accomplished composer. The two men collaborated together to compose *Break Forth, O Beauteous Heavenly Light*. The carol then came to the attention of Johann Sebastian Bach, who adapted its harmonies and released it in its final form in 1734.

Many details came together to bring us this carol. If not for the illness of Johann Rist, the poet may never have met his wife. If not for Elizabeth's love of music, Johann Schop might never have written the carol's tune. And except for the adaptations of a master musician, this carol may have faded into oblivion. How wonderful of God to bring these details together to remind us that confidence, joy, and eternal peace can be found in Jesus Christ, the Child of Christmas.

Break Forth, O Beauteous Heavenly Light

Break forth, O beauteous heav'nly light,
And usher in the morning;
Ye shepherds, shrink not with affright
But hear the angel's warning.
This Child, now weak in infancy,
Our confidence and joy shall be.
The pow'r of Satan breaking,
Our peace eternal making.

He comes, a Child from realms on high;
He comes, the heav'ns adoring.
He comes to earth to live and die,
A broken race restoring.
Although the King of kings is He,
He comes in deep humility;
His people to deliver
And reign in us forever.

— Johann Rist, 1641;
translation by John Troutbeck, 1885

THE VISIT BY THE SHEPHERDS

"THIS IS TOO GOOD to miss," the shepherds said to one another. "Let's go straight to Bethlehem now. Let's see for ourselves what the Lord has announced to us."

They raced into town as fast as they could and found their way to Mary and Joseph and, as they had been told, the baby, lying in a manger. Trembling with excitement at seeing the baby, the shepherds poured out the story the angel had told them about this child.

All the people listened, astonished. As for Mary, she treasured it all in her heart and kept thinking about it, but said nothing.

The shepherds eventually returned to their flocks, glorifying and praising God for all that they had heard and seen, just as the angels had told them.

LUKE 2:15-20

First published in 1867, this beautiful spiritual was probably written in the late eighteenth or early nineteenth century. Its authorship is uncertain, but its American origins are assured.

Since the tune fits the natural cadence of someone walking slowly, *Rise Up, Shepherd, and Follow* was often sung as men and women trudged home from work. As in other black spirituals, a soloist would sing the main line while others responded with the key phrase, *Rise up, shepherd, and follow*. And as they walked and sang, they would leave their cares behind, just as the shepherds were urged to leave their flocks, and find, instead, the Savior.

Rise Up, Shepherd, and Follow

There's a star in the east on Christmas morn.
Rise up, shepherd, and follow.
It will lead to the place where the Savior's born
Rise up, shepherd, and follow.
If you take good heed to the angel's word,
Rise up, shepherd, and follow.
You'll forget your flock; you'll forget your herd.
Rise up, shepherd, and follow.

Leave your ewes and leave your lambs.
Rise up, shepherd, and follow.
Leave your sheep and leave your rams.
Rise up, shepherd, and follow.
Follow, follow, follow the star of Bethlehem
Rise up, shepherd, and follow.

— Anonymous black spiritual

From the beginning of the Reformation until the dawn of the eighteenth century, congregational singing consisted almost entirely of versified settings of the book of Psalms. Then in 1696, during the benevolent reign of William and Mary, two Irishmen, Nahum Tate and Nicholas Brady, collaborated in undertaking a new metrical version of the Psalms that was more in keeping with the liturgical tastes of their time. This new Psalter was officially endorsed by King William III and was adopted by the Church of England, and almost a century later by the American Episcopal Church.

In 1750, Tate and Brady published a supplement to their new songbook, which contained sixteen hymns for children. One of the original hymns was *While Shepherds Watched Their Flocks*. Found in almost every Protestant hymnal, this lively hymn ranks as one of our most popular carols. Even young children can easily visualize its pure, narrative account about the shepherds.

The tune was adapted from the work of George Frederic Handel, best known for his oratorio *The Messiah*.

In the retelling of this carol's Christmas story, the shepherds followed the angel's command and went to the stable. No one else witnessed the miracle of Christ's birth. No one else in Bethlehem came to see the child. As we take time this season to listen to the angels' message, as the shepherds did, we too find God's gift of peace.

While Shepherds Watched

While shepherds watched their flocks by night,
All seated on the ground,
The angel of the Lord came down.
And glory shone around.

"Fear not," said he, (for mighty dread
Had seized their troubled mind);
"Glad tidings of great joy I bring
To you and all mankind."

"To you, in David's town, this day
Is born of David's line
A Savior, who is Christ the Lord;
And this shall be the sign:"

"The heavenly Babe you there shall find
To human view displayed,
All meanly wrapped in swathing bands,
And in a manger laid."

"All glory be to God on high,
And to the earth be peace;
Good-will henceforth, from heaven to men
Begin, and never cease."

— Nahum Tate, 1700

Adeste Fideles, as this tune is called, are the Latin words that begin the carol *O Come, All Ye Faithful.* John Francis Wade wrote the original Latin hymn in the middle of the eighteenth century. A transplanted Englishman living in Douay, France (which had earlier given birth to the Douay English Bible), Wade was a musician and skilled calligrapher. He made his living copying music for use in Roman Catholic chapels. Seven manuscript copies of his now-famous Christmas carol have been discovered, each bearing Wade's signature.

Unlike the Latin text that rhymed, the English translation made by Frederick Oakley in 1841 has irregular lines and no consistent rhyme. The music is simple, unsophisticated, but easily sung—making this one of our most frequently requested Christmas carols.

Since the carol originated in Latin, many nationalities have joyously embraced it. Because of its worldwide acceptance, *O Come, All Ye Faithful* is an international carol that reminds us that everyone may hear the good news of Christ's coming. Sharing the story of Christ's birth with others is one way we can truly come, and adore him.

O Come, All Ye Faithful

O come, all ye faithful, joyful and triumphant,
O come ye, O come ye to Bethlehem!
Come and behold Him, born the King of angels;
O come, let us adore Him, O come, let us adore Him,
O come, let us adore Him, Christ the Lord.

Sing, choirs of angels, sing in exultation!
Sing, all ye citizens of heaven above;
Glory to God, all glory in the highest;
O come, let us adore Him, O come, let us adore Him,
O come, let us adore Him, Christ the Lord.

Yea, Lord, we greet Thee, born this happy morning,
Jesus, to Thee be all glory given;
Word of the Father, now in flesh appearing;
O come, let us adore Him, O come, let us adore Him,
O come, let us adore Him, Christ the Lord.

— John F. Wade, 1751

This carol dates from the sixteenth century and quite possibly originated with a performing troupe from London. In fact, it is this very carol that appears in Charles Dickens' Christmas story, *A Christmas Carol*. A young London caroler stood outside the countinghouse of Ebenezer Scrooge and sang this carol while hoping for a penny for his purse. Though the song boasts a lively melody, this exquisite carol is spiritual in nature as it recounts the tale of the birth of Christ.

The words of **God Rest Ye Merry, Gentlemen** remind us that there were very few witnesses to this miraculous occurrence in Bethlehem. Only a small band of shepherds heard these "tidings of comfort and joy." Only the parents joined them as they worshiped the Christ child in the manger. Everyone else in Bethlehem missed that first Christmas. Some were busy. Some were sleeping. Some were too preoccupied to notice what was going on. They missed the miracle of Christmas, as many still do.

God Rest Ye Merry, Gentlemen

God rest ye merry, gentlemen,
Let nothing you dismay,
Remember Christ our Savior
Was born on Christmas Day,
To save us all from Satan's pow'r
When we were gone astray.

From God our Heavenly Father,
A blessed angel came,
And unto certain shepherds
Brought tidings of the same:
How that in Bethlehem was born
The Son of God by name.

"Fear not, then," said the angel,
"Let nothing you affright,
This day is born a Savior
Of a pure Virgin bright,
To free all those who trust in Him
From Satan's pow'r and might."

O tidings of comfort and joy, comfort and joy,
O tidings of comfort and joy.

— Author unknown

St. Columb's Cathedral in Londonderry, Northern Ireland, occupies the highest ground within the old, walled city. Most of the walls of the chapter house are lined with relics dating back to the time of the 1680s siege by King James II. Chief among the memorabilia is the portrait of a woman, saintly of face, modest of dress, and gracious of spirit.

Cecil Francis Alexander, the woman in the portrait, is still fondly remembered there. Though she died in 1895, a beautiful stained-glass window pays eloquent tribute to Mrs. Alexander's life and music in its depiction of the Savior's love and care for children. A plain, marble cross marks her resting place, and beneath her name is inscribed in brackets "Hymn Writer."

Today Cecil Francis Alexander is best remembered for her songs written especially for children, among them *All Things Bright and Beautiful*, and **Once in Royal David's City**, which she wrote in 1848. Henry J. Gauntlett, an English organist and composer, created the tune the following year.

As early as 1848, the year that she wrote **Once in Royal David's City**, Mrs. Alexander published *Hymns for Little Children*, containing forty-one hymns for the spiritual education of her young friends. Included in this book was this favorite Christmas carol. To impress spiritual lessons upon the youngsters' hearts, Mrs. Alexander made sure that each hymn focused on a section of the catechism. **Once in Royal David's City** gently reminds listeners— young and old alike—to worship God like the shepherds did. With godly determination and a sense of urgency, the shepherds dropped everything they were doing to follow the angel's command and attend Christ's birth.

Once in Royal David's City

Once in royal David's city
Stood a lowly cattle shed,
Where a mother laid her Baby
In a manger for His bed.
Mary was that mother mild,
Jesus Christ her little Child.

He came down to earth from heaven
Who is God and Lord of all,
And His shelter was a stable,
And His cradle was a stall.
With the poor and mean and lowly,
Lived on earth our Savior holy.

For He is our childhood's pattern:
Day by day like us He grew;
He was little, weak and helpless;
Tears and smiles like us He knew;
And He feeleth for our sadness,
And He shareth in our gladness.

Not in that poor lowly stable,
With the oxen standing by
We shall see Him, but in heaven,
Set at God's right hand on high,
When like stars, His children crown'd
All in white shall wait around.

— Cecil F. Alexander, 1848

The French text of this beloved Christmas carol was written by Placide Cappeau in 1847 and translated shortly thereafter from French to English by John Sullivan Dwight, an American clergyman. Cappeau, a wine merchant and mayor of a small town in southern France, wrote many poems for his own enjoyment. With his new composition in hand, Cappeau traveled to Paris to visit the celebrated classical composer Adolphe Adam, best known for his ballet *Giselle*. The musician consented to write a tune to go with Cappeau's completed Christmas poem. The carol premiered that year at Cappeau's home church, but local religious authorities denounced it for its lack of musical taste and total absence of the spirit of religion!

Despite their derogatory words, **O Holy Night!** has endured as the greatest Christmas song to come from France. Its words point to the real reason that the three kings came to visit the Christ child. The baby born on that holy night would one day grow up to suffer and die for everyone in the world. Though their gifts of gold, frankincense, and myrrh were wonderful, Jesus' gift to the kings and to us is greater still—the gift of eternal life.

O Holy Night!

O holy night! the stars are brightly shining,
It is the night of the dear Savior's birth!
Long lay the world in sin and error pining,
Till He appeared and the soul felt its worth.
A thrill of hope—the weary world rejoices,
For yonder breaks a new and glorious morn!
Fall on your knees! O hear the angel voices!
O night divine, O night when Christ was born.
O night divine! O night, O night divine!

Led by the light of faith serenely beaming,
With glowing hearts by His cradle we stand.
Led by the light of a star sweetly gleaming,
Here came the wise men from Orient land.
The King of kings lay in a lowly manger,
In all our trials born to be our Friend.
He knows our need—to our weakness He's no stranger.
Behold your King, before Him lowly bend!
Behold your King, before Him lowly bend!

— Placide Cappeau, 1847;
translation by John S. Dwight

If she cannot afford a lamb,
then she shall take two turtledoves
or two young pigeons,
    the one for a burnt offering
    and the other for a sin offering;
And the priest shall make atonement for her,
    and she shall be clean.

From the Law of Moses, c. 1440 B.C.
LEVITICUS 12:8

THE TEMPLE VISIT

THE BABY was circumcised when he was eight days old and named Jesus, the name given by the angel before he was conceived.

When the time came, according to the Mosaic Law for his mother's purification and his dedication to God, his parents took Jesus to Jerusalem.

It is written in the law of the Lord, "Every firstborn male that opens the womb shall be called holy to the Lord." And so they came to offer a sacrifice also in accordance to what was said in the law of the Lord: "A pair of turtledoves or two young pigeons."

LUKE 2:21-24

The People That in Darkness Sat

The people that in darkness sat
A glorious Light have seen.
The Light has shined on them who long
In shades of night have been.

For unto us a Child is born,
To us a Son is given.
And on His shoulders ever rests
All power in earth and heaven.

His name shall be the Prince of Peace,
Forevermore adored,
The Wonderful, the Counselor,
The great and mighty Lord.

Lord Jesus, reign in us, we pray,
And make us Thine alone,
Who with the Father ever art,
And Holy Spirit, one.

— Scottish paraphrase by John Morison, 1781

THE TESTIMONY OF SIMEON

IN JERUSALEM was a man named Simeon. This man was deeply religious, dedicated to the service of God, filled with God's Holy Spirit, and living in the expectation of the imminent salvation of Israel. Each day Simeon expected that the Messiah would appear, because the Holy Spirit had promised him that he would see the Messiah before he died.

On this particular day, prompted by God, Simeon went into the temple. When Mary and Joseph brought Jesus to dedicate him according to the custom of the law, Simeon took Jesus into his arms, blessed God, and prayed:

> "Now Lord, let your servant depart in peace,
> I am content to die.
> For you kept your word.
> My eyes have witnessed your salvation
>   which you have prepared
>   in the presence of all mankind,
> A light to reveal the unknown
>   to the Gentiles,
> A light to bring glory
>   to your people Israel."

Joseph and Mary marveled at what Simeon said about their son. Simeon then blessed them both, and turned to Mary his mother:

> "Behold, this child is destined
>   for the fall and rise of many in Israel;
> And to establish a standard
>   that many will oppose.
> Because he will reveal
>   men's true motives.
> A sword will also pierce
>   your own soul, Mary."

LUKE 2:25-35

THE TESTIMONY OF ANNA

ALSO IN THE TEMPLE at the same time was a prophetess, Anna, the daughter of Phanuel, a descendant of Asher. She was very old, a widow of eighty-four years whose husband died only seven years after they were married.

The temple had become her home. She never left it, for she worshiped, fasted, and prayed at all hours of the day and night.

At the very moment Simeon was blessing the child, she came up and also gave thanks to God. Then she told all those who were looking for the redemption of Jerusalem that she had seen Jesus, the Messiah.

Then Joseph and Mary and Jesus returned to their home in Bethlehem.

LUKE 2:36-38

Suffering touched every American family during the Civil War. Among the survivors of that dreadful conflict was Henry Wadsworth Longfellow's son, Charles. Charles Longfellow had served in the Massachusetts Regiment of the Union Army, but before the war ended, Charles was mustered out, wounded but alive. At Christmas that year, in his honor, his father wrote the verses to *I Heard the Bells on Christmas Day*.

Although the Civil War in 1864 was nearing its conclusion, Longfellow contrasted the angel's message on that first Christmas of "peace on earth, good will to men" with the horrors of war, the strength of hate, and the absence of peace on earth during the 1860s. Echoing the cry of every heart, the last two stanzas of the carol most sharply draw that contrast as they reverberate with the heartache that accompanies the hardships of war and of life. But in the final stanza Longfellow strongly affirms his and our bedrock faith: "God is not dead"; his peace will prevail.

I Heard the Bells on Christmas Day

I heard the bells on Christmas day
Their old familiar carols play,
And wild and sweet the words repeat
Of peace on earth, good will to men.

I thought how, as the day had come,
The belfries of all Christendom
Had roll'd along the unbroken song
Of peace on earth, good will to men.

And in despair I bowed my head;
"There is no peace on earth," I said,
"For hate is strong, and mocks the song
Of peace on earth, good will to men."

Then pealed the bells more loud and deep:
"God is not dead, nor doth He sleep:
The wrong shall fail, the right prevail,
With peace on earth, good will to men."

— Henry W. Longfellow, 1864

The kings of Tarshish and of the isles
    shall bring presents;
The kings of Sheba and Seb
    shall offer gifts
And he shall live,
    and to him shall be given
    the gold of Sheba:
Prayer also shall be made
    for him continually;
    and daily shall he be praised.

By King Solomon, c. 950 B.C.
PSALM 72:10, 15

The multitude of camels
    shall cover you,
    the dromedaries of Midian and Ephah;
    all they from Sheba shall come:
They shall bring gold and incense;
    and they shall show forth
    the praises of the Lord.

By the prophet Isaiah, c. 690 B.C.
ISAIAH 60:6

THE VISIT BY THE MAGI

SOMETIME LATER, still during the reign of Herod over Judea, Magi arrived in Jerusalem from the east.

"Where is he who has been born King of the Jews?" they inquired. "We saw his star in the east, and have come to pay him homage."

Of course, when Herod the king heard about this, it concerned him. In fact, it created apprehension throughout the city. So Herod assembled all the chief priests and scribes and questioned them where the Messiah was to be born.

"In Bethlehem," they told him, and quoted the prophecy:

> "And you Bethlehem,
>   in the land of Judah,
>   are by no means least
>   among the cities of Judah.
> For a ruler shall come from you
>   to govern my people Israel."

Then Herod summoned the Magi to a private meeting, and by questioning them was able to determine when the star first appeared.

Then he sent them to Bethlehem, saying: "Go and conduct a careful search for the child. When you have found him, report back to me and I'll come and join you and worship him with you."

Having heard the king, they left Jerusalem and followed the star on to Bethlehem until it stopped right above the house where the Christ child was now living.

As they watched the star, it stopped. They were ecstatic with joy. Entering the house, they saw the child with his mother Mary. Immediately they dropped to their knees and worshiped him.

From their travel bags they took their treasures—gifts made of gold and containers filled with the fragrances of frankincense and myrrh.

When the Magi left Bethlehem for their home, they deliberately bypassed Jerusalem and returned by a different route, having been warned in a dream to avoid Herod.

MATTHEW 2:1-12

But you, Bethlehem Ephratah,
    though you be little
    among the thousands of Judah,
Yet out of you shall he come forth unto me
    that is to be ruler in Israel;
Whose goings forth
    have been from old,
    from everlasting.

By the prophet Micah, c. 730 B.C.
MICAH 5:2

John Henry Hopkins, Jr. was an Episcopalian clergyman. It was his custom to send a present to his nephews and nieces in Vermont at Christmastime. But in 1857 Hopkins's personal resources were limited. Though he had tried to sell a few short stories and articles to make some extra money, none of the newspapers showed any interest. Even his artwork sat unsold in a local gallery.

As Hopkins sat at his well-worn desk, he recalled the Bible story of the three kings who followed a star to find the Christ child of Bethlehem. He began to write, *"We Three Kings of Orient Are . . ."* and his nephews and nieces were thrilled with their unique Christmas gift.

But Hopkins wasn't finished with his composition. Shortly after sending the poem to his young relatives, Hopkins wrote a haunting melody to accompany the verses. He offered the entire carol to the General Theological Seminary of New York's Christmas pageant that year. Since that time, this Episcopalian uncle's gift has become a beloved Christmas carol, with its story of hope guiding us all to the perfect light of Christ.

We Three Kings

We three kings of Orient are;
Bearing gifts we traverse afar—
Field and fountain, moor and mountain,
Following yonder star.

Born a King on Bethlehem's plain;
Gold I bring to crown Him again,
King forever, ceasing never
Over us all to reign.

Frankincense to offer have I;
Incense owns a Deity nigh.
Prayer and praising, all men raising,
Worship Him, God on high.

Glorious now behold Him arise
King, and God, and Sacrifice,
Alleluia, alleluia!
Heaven and earth replies.

O star of wonder, star of night,
Star with royal beauty bright;
Westward leading, still proceeding,
Guide us to Thy perfect light.

— John H. Hopkins, Jr.

The observance of Epiphany commemorates the visitation of the three kings to the Bethlehem home of Jesus. It was the first time the Messiah was manifested to the Gentiles.

On Epiphany Sunday in 1858, William Chatterton Dix, then only twenty-one years old, was at home recovering from a serious illness. As he read through Matthew's account of the kings' visit to Jesus, he was inspired to write **As With Gladness Men of Old.**

Magi originally referred to Persian astrologers. However, that original definition had been broadened to identify men of great wisdom, teachers and philosophers. In the second century in Rome, the great Christian historian anointed the Magi "kings" by identifying them as a fulfillment of Isaiah's prophecy that kings bringing gifts would come to Israel.

When the kings arrived in Bethlehem to pay him homage, Jesus was no longer a baby but was a child "under the age of two." Scripture also tells us that he was no longer in a manger in a stable, but in a "house."

Although William Dix twice refers to the baby Jesus in the manger bed, his slight deviation from the biblical account has not lessened our enthusiasm for his celebratory carol. His references to the costly treasures from the three kings remind us that we, too, may worship Christ by giving the King of kings the very best of our lives.

As With Gladness Men of Old

As with gladness men of old
Did the guiding star behold.
As with joy they hailed its light,
Leading onward, beaming bright;
So, most gracious Lord, may we
Evermore be led to Thee.

As with joyful steps they sped
To that lowly manger bed,
There to bend the knee before
Him whom heaven and earth adore;
So, may we with willing feet
Ever seek the mercy seat.

As they offered gifts most rare
At Thy cradle rude and bare;
So may we with holy joy,
Pure, and free from sin's alloy,
All our costliest treasures bring,
Christ, to Thee, our heavenly King.

— William C. Dix, 1858

*B*orn in Bristol, England, William Chatterton Dix's middle name was derived from the poet Thomas Chatterton. Dix's father, a surgeon, wrote a biography of the poet and in his honor gave his son this unusual middle name.

When William Dix finished school, he took a job managing a marine insurance office in Glasgow, Scotland. His heart, however, found its voice in the poetry of worship. In addition to compiling several songbooks, Dix wrote more than 40 hymns. He composed *What Child Is This?* around 1865. The folk melody *Greensleeves*, which frames the tune for this carol, was most likely created in the sixteenth century in England during the time of William Shakespeare. This serene carol fills all who sing it with a gentle peace, reminding us that those who visited the Christ child came willingly to worship and were filled with joy at finding the Babe, the son of Mary.

What Child Is This?

What Child is this, who, laid to rest,
On Mary's lap is sleeping?
Whom angels greet with anthems sweet,
While shepherds watch are keeping?
This, this is Christ the King,
Whom shepherds guard and angels sing:
Haste, haste to bring him laud, The Babe, the son of Mary.

Why lies He in such mean estate
Where ox and ass are feeding?
Good Christian, fear; for sinners here
The silent Word is pleading.
Raise, raise the song on high;
The virgin sings her lullaby.
Joy, joy, for Christ is born—The Babe, the son of Mary.

— William C. Dix, 1865

I see Him, but not now;
    I behold Him, but not near.
a Star shall come out of Jacob;
    a Scepter shall rise out of Israel.

From the Law of Moses, c. 1400 B.C.
NUMBERS 24:17

THE ESCAPE TO EGYPT

SHORTLY AFTER the Magi had departed, Joseph had a dream in which an angel of the Lord warned, "Rise up quickly! Take the child and his mother; flee to Egypt, and remain there until I tell you. For Herod is preparing to search for the child to destroy him!"

Joseph got up and woke Mary. They hurriedly packed together some of their belongings and left for Egypt that night. They remained there until Herod died.

Once more a prophecy was fulfilled, for Hosea had written: "I summoned my son out of Egypt."

Meanwhile, when Herod had not received a report from the Magi, he realized he had been tricked. In a furious rage he ordered his men to kill all the baby boys under the age of two in Bethlehem and all that vicinity. (He calculated the age at two based on what the Magi had told him.)

In this, a prediction of the prophet was fulfilled:

> "A voice is heard in Ramah,
>   an anguished wail of mourning.
> Rachael weeps for her children:
>   bereft beyond all consolation
>   because her children lie dead."

MATTHEW 2:13-18

"When Israel was a child,
      then I loved him;
And called my son
      out of Egypt."

By the prophet Hosea, c. 720 B.C.
HOSEA 11:1

"Thus says the Lord:
      A voice was heard in Ramah,
      lamentation,
      and bitter weeping;
Rachael weeping for her children
      refused to be comforted for her children,
      because they were not."

By the prophet Jeremiah, c. 590 B.C.
JEREMIAH 31:15

THE BOYHOOD OF JESUS

Home to Nazareth

Jesus in the Temple

Back in Nazareth

HOME TO NAZARETH

AFTER HEROD DIED, an angel of the Lord again appeared to Joseph in a dream.

"It is time to go home now," the angel announced. "Take the child and his mother and go into the land of Israel. For those who attempted to murder the child are dead."

Joseph immediately took the child and his mother, left Egypt, and returned to the land of Israel.

As they neared the border, Joseph heard that Herod had been succeeded in Judea by his son Archelaus. This made Joseph afraid, and being warned in yet another dream, he skirted Judea and settled instead in a town in Galilee called Nazareth. So the prophecies again were fulfilled when they said of the Messiah: "He shall be called a Nazarene."

It was in Nazareth that Jesus grew up. As he grew, he became spiritually strong, increasing in wisdom beyond his years. The grace of God was clearly on his young life.

MATTHEW 2:19-23; LUKE 2:39-40

JESUS IN THE TEMPLE

THE CUSTOM of Jesus' parents was to go to Jerusalem each year for the Passover. When he was twelve years old, they took Jesus along.

When the festival was over, Mary and Joseph started back to Nazareth, assuming that Jesus was with other relatives or friends in the caravan. It was not until they had traveled all day, and the caravan had stopped for the night, that Mary and Joseph realized he was lost and began frantically searching for him.

When he was nowhere to be found, they returned to Jerusalem, searching for him everywhere along the road and in the city.

Three days later they finally found him. There he was, sitting among the teachers of the law, listening to them, asking them questions, astonishing them all with his understanding and with his answers. Even his parents were astonished.

Then it was his mother's turn to ask questions: "Son, why have you treated your father and me like this? We have been anxiously looking everywhere for you! Did you not realize that we have been worried sick?"

Jesus responded to his parents: **"Why were you searching all over for me? Did you not know that I had to be right here in my Father's house?"**

But they did not fully understand his reply.

Luke 2:41-50

BACK IN NAZARETH

THEN HE RETURNED home to Nazareth and was an obedient son to them. His mother treasured all these early experiences.

As for Jesus, he grew older, taller, and wiser, popular with God and among his friends.

LUKE 2:51-52

Sing We Now of Christmas

Sing we now of Christmas, Noel sing we here!
Listen to our praises to the Babe so dear.
Sing we Noel,
The King is born, Noel!
Sing we now of Christmas, sing we all Noel!

Shepherds on the hillside heard the angels sing:
Glory, honor, praises, to the infant King.
Sing we Noel,
The King is born, Noel!
Sing we now of Christmas, sing we all Noel!

Wise Men sought and found Him, treasures did they bring;
Bowing down they worshiped Christ, the King of kings.
Sing we Noel,
The King is born, Noel!
Sing we now of Christmas, sing we all Noel!

— Traditional French carol;
stanzas 2-3 by Tom Fettke

This wonderfully bright traditional English folksong, written by William Sandys, was first published in 1835 in *Christmas Carols Ancient and Modern*. Richard Beckley was the publisher.

In *I Saw Three Ships*, which reflects Great Britain's maritime heritage, we find ourselves focusing upon a flotilla sailing into Bethlehem to celebrate the birth of our Savior.

The carol's message clearly reflects the original story, as the angels, joined by the bells of Christmas, lead us in this gleeful, joyful, happy celebration.

I Saw Three Ships

I saw three ships come sailing in.
On Christmas day, on Christmas day;
I saw three ships come sailing in,
On Christmas day in the morning.
And what was in those ships all three,
On Christmas day, on Christmas day?
And what was in those ships all three.
On Christmas day in the morning?

The Virgin Mary and Christ were there,
On Christmas day, on Christmas day;
The Virgin Mary and Christ were there,
On Christmas day in the morning.
And all the bells on earth shall ring,
On Christmas day, on Christmas day;
And all the bells on earth shall ring,
On Christmas day in the morning.

And all the Angels in Heaven shall sing,
On Christmas day, on Christmas day;
And all the Angels in Heaven shall sing,
On Christmas day in the morning.
Then let us all rejoice again,
On Christmas day, on Christmas day;
Then let us all rejoice again,
On Christmas day in the morning.

— Traditional English folksong;
William Sandys, 1835

INDEX TO SCRIPTURES

ALPHABETICAL INDEX OF SONGS

ACKNOWLEDGMENTS

Carmichael, Ralph, et.al. *The New Church Hymnal.* Wichita, KS: Lexicon Music, Inc., 1976.

The Christmas Card Songbook. Milwaukee, WI: Hal Leonard Publishing Corporation, 1991

Fettke, Tom, et.al. *The Celebration Hymnal: Song and Hymns for Worship.* Dallas, TX: Word Music / Integrity Music, 1997.

Hustad, Donald P., ed. *Hymns for the Living Church.* Carol Stream, IL: Hope Publishing Company, 1981.

Osbeck, Kenneth W. *101 Hymn Stories: The Inspiring True Stories Behind 101 Favorite Hymns.* Grand Rapids, MI: Kregel Publications, 1982.

101 More Hymn Stories: The Inspiring True Stories Behind 101 Favorite Hymns. Grand Rapids, MI: Kregel Publications, 1985.

Peterson, John W. and Norman Johnson. *Praise! Our Songs and Hymns.* C.B.A. Special Edition. Grand Rapids, MI: Singspiration Music of the Zondervan Corporation, 1979.

Reynolds, William J. *Songs of Glory: Stories of 300 Great Hymns and Gospel Songs.* Grand Rapids, MI: Baker Books, 1990.

Internet Resources:
The Cyber Hymnal: www.cyberhymnal.org
Chris Hill: www.christmas-community.com/carols
Montrose Music: www3.pair.com/montrsmu/carolshist